IN

THEIR

OWN

WORDS

IN
THEIR
OWN
WORDS

P. J. Green

Publisher: Green's Corner

Cover Design: Mystic Circle Designs
Cover/Interior Images: Courtesy of Pixabay

ISBN: 978-1-7328710-0-7

Dedication

I want to give my thanks to my ancestors who allowed me to be so blessed as to born here in the United States. My ancestors who came from: Ireland, England, France, and many other countries too numerous to mention.

They were the Gambles of South Carolina and Mississippi, the Paschal's of Arkansas and Tennessee, Younce's of Arkansas, and the Cameron's of South Carolina. I am forever indebted to them.

Acknowledgements

I can't write a book without recognizing my parents:
Phillip Joseph Paschal, Jr. and
Stella Jeanette (Gamble) Paschal.

Also, my appreciation to my husband Bob Green, who has day
after day allowed me to close my door and work all hours on
my writings.

To our son, Christopher Brian Green, who is our pride and joy.

To his wife, April Burleson Green, who is the answer to so
many of our prayers.

This is especially written for my younger brother,
Thomas K. Paschal.

Introduction

Recently I have been asking myself how much I really know about our Founding Fathers thoughts and fears with regards to this new land called America. Below I have listed some of these insights—most still relevant today. You will find many more within this book.

Enjoy!!!!

George Washington's true faith can be found in the following quote:

"Bless my family, kindred, friends and country, be our God and guide this day and forever for His sake, who lay down in the grave and arose again for us, Jesus Christ our Lord. Amen."

James Madison quoted the old Testament Isaiah 33:22 to form what he thought would be a perfect government:

For the Lord is our judge—our justice department

For the Lord is our lawgiver—congress

For the Lord is our king—president—executive

John Adams upon signing the constitution expressed the fact that he knew many would die to safeguard it.

"I am well aware of the Toil and Blood and Treasure, that it will cost us to maintain this Declaration, and support and defend these states."

Thomas Jefferson spoke many times about the importance

of money and fame. Below is one such quote:

"Give up money, give up fame, give up science, give up the earth itself and all it contains rather than do an immoral act."

Martin Van Buren expressed concern about the national debt in the following quote:

"In time of peace there can, at all events, be no justification for the creation of a permanent debt by the Federal Government."

Abraham Lincoln is attributed to the following quote:

"If you once forfeit the confidence of your fellow citizens, you can never regain their respect and esteem. It is true that you may fool all the people some of the time; you can even fool some of the people all the time; but you can't fool all the people all the time."

Andrew Jackson gave credit to the hand of Providence for his success in the Battle of New Orleans:

"It appears the unerring hand of Providence shielded my men from the shower of balls, bombs, and rockets."

Regarding public employees **Grover Cleveland** stated the following:

"Our citizens have the right to protection from the incompetency of public employees who hold their places solely as the reward of partisan service."

"Officeholders are the agents of the people, not their masters."

Benjamin Harrison regarding cheap goods:

"I pity the man who wants a coat so cheap that the man or woman who produces the cloth will starve in the process."

William McKinley had the following thoughts regarding government spending:

"The best way for the government to maintain its credit is to pay as it goes."

Woodrow Wilson was concerned about materialism:

"Our civilization cannot survive materially unless it be redeemed spiritually with the Spirit of Christ."

Warren G. Harding regarding God said:

"It is my conviction that the fundamental trouble with the people of the United States is that they have gotten too far away from Almighty God."

Calvin Coolidge regarding the senate:

"I soon found that the Senate had but one fixed rule, subject to exceptions of course, which was to the effect that the Senate would do anything it wanted to do whenever it wanted to do it."

Herbert Hoover regarding taxes stated:

"The budget should be balanced not by more taxes, but ty reduction of follies."

Truman regarding the subject of polls Truman stated:

"I wonder how far Moses would have gotten if he had taken a poll in Egypt?"

Table of Contents

1789 - 1797

George Washington

Character

"It should be the highest ambition of every American to extend his views beyond himself, and to bear in mind that his conduct will not only affect himself, his country, and his immediate posterity; but that its influence may be co-extensive with the world and stamp political happiness or misery on ages yet unborn." (Letter to the Legislature of Pennsylvania, September 5, 1789)

"I now make it my earnest prayer that God would have you and the citizens of your states entertain a brotherly affection and love for one another particularly for those who have served in the field." (*The Model for Presidential Character—George Washington*—The Patriot Post)

"The General hopes and trusts that every officer and man will endeavor to live, and act as becomes a Christian soldier defending the dearest rights and liberties of his country." (*The Writings of George Washington*" p.401)

God

"Oh, eternal and everlasting God, direct my thoughts, words and work. Wash away my sins in the immaculate blood of the lamb and purge my heart by the Holy Spirit."

"I have often expressed my sentiments, that every man, conducting himself as a good citizen, and being accountable to God alone for his religious opinion, ought to be protected in worshipping the Deity according to the dictates of his own conscience." (Letter to the General Committee of the United Baptist Churches in Virginia: May 1789)

"We have abundant reason to rejoice that in this land that every person may have worshiped God according to the dictates of his conscience." (Letter to New Jerusalem Church—in Newport, Rhode Island: 8/18/1790)

Military/War/Patriots

"Discipline is the soul of an army. It makes small numbers formidable; procures success to the weak, and esteem to all." (Letter of Instructions to the Captains of the Virginia Regiments: Washington's prayer book: July 29, 1759)

"The fate of unborn millions will now depend, under God, on the courage and conduct of this army. We have therefore to resolve to conquer or die." (August 27, 1776: Address to the Continental Army before the Battle of Long Island)

"The General is sorry to be informed that the foolish and wicked practice of profane cursing and swearing, heretofore little known in the army is growing into fashion. He hopes the officers will, by example as well as by influence, endeavor to check it." (Order issued by George Washington—to officers during the Revolution War)

In His Prayer Book

"Bless my family, kindred, friends and country, be our God and guide this day and forever for His sake, who lay down in the grave and arose again for us, Jesus Christ our Lord. Amen." (Washington's Prayers)

"Refrain from drink which is the source of all evil-and the ruin of half the workmen in this Country." (Letters and Addresses)

Humanity

"Happy, thrice happy shall they who have assisted in protecting the rights of human nature and establishing an Asylum for the poor and oppressed of all nations and religions." (General Orders: April 18, 1783)

"I have often expressed my sentiments, that every man, conducting himself as a good citizen, and being accountable to God alone for his religious opinion, ought to be protected in worshipping the Deity according to the dictates of his own conscience." (Letter to the General Committee of the United Baptist Churches in Virginia: May 1789)

1797 - 1801

John Adams

Character

"The foundation of national morality must be laid in private families. How is It possible that children can have any just sense of the sacred obligations of morality or religion if, from their earliest infancy, they learn their Mothers live in habitual infidelity to their fathers, and their fathers in as constant infidelity to their Mothers?" (Diary: June 2, 1778)

"To be good, and to do good, is all we have to do." (*What the Founding Fathers Said about Success Will Change Your Approach to Life*: September 17, 2013)

"The happiness of man, as well as his dignity, consists in virtue." (Letters Addressed to His Wife: p.277)

"But, my dear boy, above all things, preserve your innocence, and a pure conscience. Your morals are of more importance, both to yourself and the world than all languages and all sciences. The least stain upon your character will do more harm to your happiness than all accomplishments will do it good." (John Adams to John Quincy Adams: April 28, 1782, in Adams Family Correspondence, vol. 4, ed. L. H. Butterfield, Cambridge, Mass.: The Belknap Press of Harvard University Press, 1973: p.317)

Constitution, Government

John Adams: July 1, 1776

"Before God, I believe the hour has come. My Judgment approves this measure, and my whole heart is in it. All that I have, and all that I am, and all that I hope in this life, I am now ready here to stake upon it." (Passing of the Constitution)

God

"I now believe, that those general principles of Christianity are as eternal and immutable as the existence of attributes of God." (Letter to Thomas Jefferson: June 28, 1813)

"The Ten Commandments and the Sermon on the Mount contain my religion." (Letter from John Adams to Thomas Jefferson: November 4, 1816)

"Without religion this world would be something not fit to be mentioned in polite company, I mean hell." (Letter from John Adams to Thomas Jefferson: April 19, 1817)

"It is the duty of all men in society, publicly, and at stated seasons, to worship the Supreme Being." (Thoughts on Government: 1776)

"We have no government armed with power capable of contending with human passions unbridled by morality and religion." (Speech to the Military: 1798)

"The right to freedom being the gift of God Almighty." (Rights of the Colonists: 1772)

"Suppose a nation in some distant region should take the Bible for their only law book, and every member should regulate his conduct by the precepts there exhibited. What a Eutopia, what a Paradise would this region be." (Diary on February 22, 1756)

War/Military/Veterans

"I am well aware of the toil and blood and treasure, that it will cost us to maintain this declaration, and support and defend these states." (Letter to Abigail Adams: July 3, 1776)

"The Revolution was in the minds and hearts of the people; a change in their religious sentiments, of their duties and obligations." (Letter to H. Niles: February 13, 1818)

Children & Education

"I must study politics and war that my sons may have liberty to study mathematics and philosophy." (Letter to Abigail Adams: 1780)

1801 - 1809

Thomas Jefferson

Government

"If we can prevent the government from wasting the labors of the people under the pretense of taking care of them, they must become happy." (Jefferson to Isaac Story: December 5, 1801, in PTJ, 36:30)

"I reposed my head on that pillow of ignorance which a benevolent creator has made so soft for us, knowing how much we should be forced to use it."

Lottery

"A lottery is a salutary instrument and a tax laid on the willing only, that is to say, on those who can risk the price of a ticket without sensible injury, for the possibility of a higher prize." (Memoirs, 4: Correspondence and Private Papers, p.440)

God--Thanksgiving

"The God who gave us life gave us liberty at the same time." (View of the Rights of British America, 1774)

"I have sworn upon the alter of God eternal hostility against every form of tyranny over the mind of man." (Letter to Dr. Benjamin Rush: September 23, 1800)

"And can the liberties of a nation be thought secure when we have removed their only firm basis, a conviction in the minds of the people that these liberties are the gift of God?" (Notes on the State of Virginia, Query 1781)

"I sincerely wish you will find it convenient to come here. The pleasure of the trip will be less than you expect but the utility greater. It will make you adore your own country, it's soil, it's climate. My God! how little do my country men know what precious blessings they are in possession of." (Letter to James Monroe: June 17,1785)

Character

"Give up money, give up fame, give up science, give the earth itself and all it contains rather than do an immoral act." (Letter to Peter Carr: August 19, 1785)

"Almighty God, who has given us this good land for our heritage; we humbly beseech Thee that we may always prove ourselves a people mindful of thy favor and glad to do thy will." (Letter from Thomas Jefferson to James Madison: 1823)

"I have never considered a difference of opinion in politics, in religion, in philosophy, as cause for withdrawing from a friend." (Thomas Jefferson to William Hamilton: April 22, 1800)

Toward the end of Jefferson's life, a friend asked him to write some advice to his son. (Letter from Thomas Jefferson to Thomas Jefferson Smith)

What follows is that advice:

This letter was written February 21,1825

"This letter will, to you be as one from the dead. The writer will be in the grave before you can weigh its counsels. Your affectionate and excellent father has requested that I would address something which might possibly have a favorable influence on the course of life you have to run, and I too, as a namesake, feel an interest in that course. Few words will be necessary, with good disposition on your part. Adore God. Reverence and cherish your parents. Love your neighbor as yourself, and your country more than yourself. Be just. Be true. Murmur not at the ways of Providence. And if to the dead it is permitted to care for the things of this world, every action of your life will be under my regard. Farewell."

A Decalogue of Canons for observation in practical life. Thomas Jefferson:

Never put off till tomorrow what you can do to-day.

Never trouble another for what you can do today.

Never spend your money before you have it.

Never buy what you do not want, because it is cheap; it will be dear to you.

Pride costs us more than hunger, thirst and cold.

We never repent of having eaten too little.

Nothing is troublesome that we do willingly.

How much pain have cost us the evils which have never happened.

When angry, count ten before you speak; if very angry, a hundred.

Take things always by their smooth handle.

Education

"If the children are untaught; their ignorance and vices will in future life cost us much dearer in their consequences than it would have done in their correction by a good education." (The Works of Thomas Jefferson: Correspondence and Papers, 1816-1826" p. 84, Cosimo, Inc.)

"To penetrate and dissipate these clouds of darkness, the general mind must be strengthened by education." (*Democracy*)

Taxes

"I think it is a great error to consider a heavy tax on wines as a tax on luxury. On the contrary, it is a tax on the health of our citizens." (The Works of Thomas Jefferson: Correspondence and Papers, 1816-1826", p.100, Cosimo, Inc.)

"To compel a man to furnish funds for the propagation of ideas he disbelieves and abhors is sinful and tyrannical." (The Life and Writings of Thomas Jefferson)

"The tax which will be paid for the purpose of education is not more than the thousandth part of what will be paid to kings, priests, and nobles who will rise up among us if we leave the people in ignorance." (The Life and Writings of Thomas Jefferson)

1809 - 1817

James Madison

God

"We have staked the whole future of our new nation, not upon the power of government; far from it. We have staked the future upon the capacity of each of ourselves to govern ourselves according to the moral principles of the Ten Commandments." (Given to the General Assembly of the State of Virginia: 1778)

Government

"If the laws be so voluminous that they cannot be read, or so incoherent that they cannot be understood: if they be repealed or revised before they are promulgated, or undergo such incessant changes, that no man who know what the law is today, can guess what it be tomorrow." (In the Federalist, 1788, Essay 62)

"The accumulation of all powers, legislative, executive, and judiciary, in the same hands, whether of one, a few, or many, and whether hereditary, self-appointed, or elective, may justly be pronounced the very definition of tyranny." (The Federalist no. 47: 1788)

"We are teaching the world the great truth that Governments do better without Kings and Nobles than with them." (James Madison: 1867, p.176)

"I cannot undertake to lay my finger on that article of the Constitution which granted a right to Congress of expending, on objects of benevolence, the money of their constituents." (Time Magazine: *We Don't Need No Stinking Constitution* by Larry Elder: July 7, 2011)

At the Constitutional Convention of 1787:

Madison referenced Isaiah 33:22 to form what he thought would be a perfect government:

For the Lord is our judge – our justice department

For the Lord is our lawgiver – congress

The lord is our king – president – executive

By using Isaiah 33:22 Madison formed the model of government.

Isaiah 33:22

"For the Lord is our judge, the Lord is our lawgiver, the Lord is our king; He will save us." (James Madison and the Constitution and branches of Government/*The Story of Liberty*, Author Jennifer Featherstone)

"We are teaching the world the great truth that Governments

do better without Kings and Nobles than with them." (Letter to Edward Livingston: July 10, 1822)

War and Peace

"Peace is better than war, war is better than tribute." (Letter to the Day of Algiers: August 1816)

"It is not the talking but the walking and working person that is the true Christian." (William C. Rives, *Biography of James Madison*, Vol 1, 33-34)

During the Revolution as enemy troops were heading to the White House:

James Madison's wife: Dolley Madison:

"I am accordingly ready; I have pressed as many Cabinet papers into trunks as to fill one carriage; our private property must be sacrificed, as it is impossible to procure wagons for its transportation."

"And now, dear sister, I must leave this house, or the retreating army will make me a prisoner in it by filling up the road I am directed to take." (Memoirs and Letters of Dolly Madison, Boston; New York, Houghton, Miffin)

Children, Education

Letter to the citizens of Philadelphia:

"Let the children who are sent to those schools be taught to read and write and above all, let both sexes be carefully instructed in the principles and obligations of the Christian religion. This is the most essential part of education."

"The only means of establishing and perpetuating our republican form of government is the universal education of our youth in the principles of Christianity by means of the Bible."

"The great enemy of the salvation of man, in my opinion, never invented a more effective means of limiting Christianity from the world than by persuading mankind that it was improper to read the Bible at schools."

"Knowledge will forever govern ignorance; and a people who mean to be their own governors must arm themselves with the power which knowledge gives."

1817 - 1825

James Monroe

God

"The liberty, prosperity, and the happiness of our country will always be the object of my most fervent prayers to the supreme author of all good."

(Ian Elliot, United States. President (1817-1825; Monroe : 1969)

(James Monroe, 1758-1831: chronology, documents, bibliographical aids, Oceana Pubns.)

1825 - 1829

John Quincy Adams

"The Sermon on the Mount commands me to lay up for myself treasures, not upon earth, but in Heaven. My hopes of a future life are all founded upon the Gospel of Christ." (Writings of John Quincy Adams)

"If your actions inspire others to dream more, learn more, do more and become more, you are a leader."

"From the experience of the past we derive instructive lessons for the future."

"Always vote for principle, though you vote alone, and you may cherish the sweetest reflection that your vote is never lost."

1829 - 1837

Andrew Jackson

God

"It appears the unerring hand of Providence shielded my men from the shower of balls, bombs, and rockets, when every ball and bomb from our guns carried with them a mission of death." (Letter written on January 8, 1815 to Robert Hays regarding the Battle of New Orleans—War of 1812)

"You have the highest of human trusts committed to your care. Providence has showered on this favored land blessings without number, and has chosen you as the guardians of freedom, to preserve it for the benefit of the human race. May He who holds in His hands the destinies of nations, make you worthy of the favors He has bestowed, and enable you, with pure hearts and hands and sleepless vigilance, to guard and defend to the end of time, the great charge He has committed to your keeping. (Federer, America's God and Country, 310)

As he was dying:

My dear children, do not grieve for me; it is true, I am going to leave you, I am well aware of my situation. I have suffered much bodily pain, but my sufferings are but as nothing compared with that which our blessed Redeemer endured upon the accursed Cross, that all might be saved who put their trust in him." (His last words on June 8, 1845 to his loved ones)

"Sir, I am in the hands of a merciful God. I have full confidence in his goodness and mercy. The Bible is true. Upon that sacred volume I rest my hope for eternal salvation." (On his death bed : May 20, 1845)

"When I have suffered sufficiently, the Lord will then take me to Himself—but what are all my sufferings compared to those of the Blessed Savior, who died upon that cursed tree for me? Mine are nothing." (Remini, Robert Vincent-Andrew Jackson and the Course of the American Empire—3 vols.)

War

"The brave man inattentive to his duty, is worth little more to his country, than the coward who deserts her in the hour of danger." (To troops who had abandoned their lines during the battle of New Orleans: January 8, 1815)

Government

"Every man is equally entitled to protection by law. But when the laws undertake to add artificial distinctions, to grant titles, gratuities, and exclusive privileges—to make the rich richer and the potent more powerful—the humble members of society—

the farmers, mechanics, and laborers, who have neither the time nor the means of securing like favors to themselves, have a right to complain of the injustice of their government."

"I am one of those who do not believe that a national debt is a national blessing, but rather a curse to a republic; inasmuch as it is calculated to raise around the administration a moneyed aristocracy dangerous to the liberties of the country." (Sam B. Smith, Harriet Fason Chappell Owsley, Harold D. Moser: 1996. *The Papers of Andrew Jackson*: 1821-1824, p.399, Univ. of Tennessee Press)

"Unless you become more watchful in your states and check the spirit of monopoly and thirst for exclusive privileges you will in the end find that the control over your dearest interests has passed into the hands of these corporations." (Messages and Papers of the Presidents: Andrew Jackson and Martin Van Buren, p. 1525, Wildside Press)

Character, Humanity

Showing Compassion: Upon hearing of the death of General Coffee:

Rely on our dear Savior. He will be father to the fatherless and husband to the widow. Trust in the mercy and goodness of Christ, and always be ready to say with heartfelt resignation, "may the Lord's will be done." (Letter to General Coffee's family—he had recently died)

When Mary and Andrew Jackson Hutchings lost their firstborn in 1834 Andrew Jackson wrote them the following:

"My dear Hutchings. I am truly happy to find that you both have met this severe bereavement with that Christian meekness and submission as was your duty. This charming babe was only given you from your Creator and benefactor. He has a right to take away, and we ought humbly to submit to His will and be always ready to say, blessed be His name. We have one consolation under this severe bereavement, that this babe is now in the bosom of its Savior."

Virtues listed in his autobiography:

Temperance: Drink not to elevation.

Silence: Avoid trifling conversation.

Order: Let all your things have their places.

Resolution: Perform with fail what you resolve.

Frugality: Waste nothing.

Industry: Lose no time.

Sincerity: Use no hurtful deceit.

Justice: Wrong none by doing injuries.

Moderation: Avoid extremes.

Tranquility: Be not disturbed at trifles.

Cleanliness: Toleration no uncleanliness in body.

Humility: Imitate Jesus.

"Happiness consists more in small conveniences of pleasures that occur every day, than in great pieces of good fortune that happen but seldom to a man during his life."

"Money never made a man happy yet, nor will it. There is nothing in its nature to produce happiness. The more a man has, the more he wants. That was a true proverb of the wise man, rely upon it: Better is little with the fear of the Lord, then great treasure, and trouble therewith."

"By failing to prepare, you are preparing to fail."

"Having been poor is no shame but being ashamed of it is."

"He does not possess wealth that allows it to possess him."

1837 - 1841

Martin Van Buren

Government Debt

"To avoid the necessity of a permanent debt and its inevitable consequences, I have advocated and endeavored to carry into effect the policy of confining the appropriations for the public service to such objects only as are clearly with the constitutional authority of the Federal Government." (*Messages and Papers of the Presidents* Martin Van Buren, William Henry Harrison, John Tyler, James K. Polk)

"There is a power in public opinion in this country—and I thank God for it: for it is the most honest and best of all powers—which will not tolerate an incompetent or unworthy man to hold in his weak or wicked hands the lives and fortunes of his fellow-citizens." (*The Complete Book of U.S. Presidents:* William A. Degregorio, p. 133)

"In time of peace there can, at all events, be no justification for the creation of a permanent debt by the Federal Government. Its limited range of constitutional duties may certainly under such circumstances be performed without such a resort." (*Messages and Papers of the Presidents*: Martin Van Buren, William Henry Harrison, John Tyler, James K. Polk", p. 1825, Wildside Press LLC)

"The less government interferes with private pursuits, the better for general prosperity." (Martin Van Buren: 1782-1862, chronology-documents-bibliographical aids)

1841 - 1841

William Henry Harrison

God

"Conscience, that vicegerent of God in the human heart, worse "still small voice" the loudest revelry cannot drown." (Christmas tales, historical and domestic, p. 187)

"Sound morals, religious liberty, and a just sense of religious responsibility are essentially connected with all true and lasting happiness."

1841 - 1845

John Tyler

God

"If we find ourselves increasing beyond example in numbers, in strength, in wealth, in knowledge, in everything which promotes human and social happiness, let us ever remember our dependence for all these on the protection and merciful dispensations of Divine Providence." (David A. Durfee, William Henry Harrison, John Tyler, United States. President: 1841-1845, Tyler, Oceana Pubns)

"Let it be henceforth proclaimed to the world that man's conscience was created free; that he is no longer accountable to his fellow man for his religious opinions, being responsible therefore only to his God." (Funeral oration for Thomas Jefferson: July 11, 1826)

1845 – 1849

James K. Polk

Government, Congress

"There is more selfishness and less principle among members of congress than I had any conception of, before I became President of the U.S."

"Thank God, under our Constitution there was no connection between church and state." (The diary of James K. Polk during his presidency, 1845 to 1849, now first printed from the original manuscript in the collections of the Chicago historical society; Vol 4, p.261.)

"The most successful politician is he who says what the people are thinking most often in the loudest voice." (View of the Rights of British America: 1774)

"I enter upon the discharge of the high duties which have been assigned me by the people, again humbly supplicating that Divine Being who has watched over and protected our beloved country from its infancy to the present hour to continue His gracious benedictions upon us, that we may continue to be a prosperous and happy people." (Closing paragraph of Inaugural Address: March 4, 1845)

1849 – 1850

Zachary Taylor

God

"The Bible is the best of books, and I wish it were in the hands of everyone. It is indispensable to the safety and permanence of our institutions. A free government cannot exist without religion and morals, and there cannot be morals without religion. Especially should the Bible be placed in the hands of the young. It is the best school book in the world." (Old Rough and Ready, Inaugural Address: March 15, 1849)

1850 – 1853

Millard Fillmore

God

"May God save the country, for it is evident that the people will not." (Letter to Henry Clay: November 11, 1844; as quoted in Presidential Wit from Washington to Johnson)

"The man who can look upon a crisis without being willing to offer himself upon the altar of his country is not fit for public trust."

"An honorable defeat is better than a dishonorable victory."

"Nothing brings out the lower traits of human nature like office seeking. Men of good character and impulses are betrayed by it into all sorts of meanness."

1853 – 1857

Franklin Pierce

God, Our Forefathers

Inaugural Address, March 4, 1853

"I can express no better hope for my country than that the kind Providence which smiled upon our fathers may enable their children to preserve the blessings they have inherited."

"It must be felt that there is no national security but, in the nation's, humble, acknowledged dependence upon God and His overruling providence." (Franklin Pierce: 1804-1869, chronology, documents, bibliographical aids)

Character

"If your past is limited, your future is boundless." (Franklin Pierce: 1804-1869; chronology, documents, bibliographical aid.)

1857 – 1861

James Buchanan

Character

"Whatever the result may be, I shall carry to my grave the consciousness that I at least meant well for my country." (Mr. Buchanan's Administration: *On the Eve of the Rebellion*, p. 296)

"All the friends that I loved and wanted to reward are dead, and all the enemies that I hated, and I had marked out for punishment are turned to my friends. (On finally achieving his country's highest political office at age 65.)

"The Government of the United States possesses no power whatever over the question of religion." (The Works of James Buchanan; Comprising His Speeches, State Papers, and Private Correspondence)

1861 – 1865

Abraham Lincoln

Character

"If you once forfeit the confidence of your fellow citizens, you can never regain their respect and esteem. It is true that you may fool all the people some of the time; you can even fool some of the people all the time; but you can't fool all of the people all of the time." (To a caller at the White House. From Alexander K. McClure, Lincoln's Yarns and Stories: 1940, p. 124)

"If I were to try to read, much less answer, all the attacks made on me, this shop might as well be closed for any other business. I do the very best I know how—the very best I can; and I mean to keep doing so until the end. If the end brings me out all right, what is said against me won't amount to anything." (Conversation at the White House. From Francis B. Carpenter, six months at the White House with Abraham Lincoln: 1866)

"I have endured a great deal of ridicule without much malice;

and have received a great deal of kindness, not quite free from ridicule. I am used to it." (Letter to James H. Hackett: November 2, 1863)

"The President last night had a dream. He was in a party of plain people and as it became known who he was they began to comment on his appearance. One of them said, 'He is a common-looking man.' The President replied, 'Common-looking people are the best in the world: that is the reason the Lord makes so many of them.'" (From letters of John Hay and Extracts from His Diary, edited by C.L. Hay: December 23, 1863)

"Nobody has ever expected me to be President. In my poor, lean, lank face nobody has ever seen that any cabbages were sprouting out." (Second campaign speech against Douglas, Springfield, Illinois: July 17,1858)

Government, Voting

"The ballot is stronger than the bullet." (Speech, Bloomington, Illinois: May 19, 1856)

God

"Let us have faith that right makes might, and in that faith let us to the end dare to do our duty as we understand it." (Address, Cooper Union, New York: February 27, 1860)

"It is difficult to make a man miserable while he feels he is worthy of himself and claim kindred to the great God who made him." (August 14, 1862)

"It may seem strange that any men should dare to ask a just

God's assistance in wringing their bread from the sweat of other men's faces, but let us judge not, that we be not judged." (Second Inaugural Address: March 4, 1865)

Inaugural Address

"Our faith teaches that there is no safer reliance than upon the God of our fathers, who has so singularly favored the American people in every national trial."

Education

"Illiteracy must be banished from the land if we shall attain that high destiny as the foremost of the enlightened nations of the world, which, under Providence, we ought to achieve."

Faith in Human Kind

"I am a firm believer in the people. If given the truth, they can be depended upon to meet any national crises. The great point is to bring them the real fact, and beer." (Post-Civil War regarding reconstruction)

1865 – 1869

Andrew Johnson

Government

"Legislation can neither be wise or just which seeks the welfare of a single interest at the expense and to the injury of many and varied interests." (*The Papers of Andrew Johnson*: September 1868-April 1869, pp.471 Tennessee Press)

"The goal to strive for is a poor government but a rich people." (*Andrew Johnson, Plebeian and Patriot*, Robert Watson Winston: 1928)

Our Flag

"Let us look forward to the time when we can take the flag of our country and nail it below the Cross, and there let it wave as it waved in the olden times, and let us gather around it and inscribed for our motto: 'Liberty and Union, one and inseparable, now and forever,' and exclaim, 'Christ first, our country next!'" (Expulsion of Mr. Bright: Speech of Hon. Andrew Johnson, of Tennessee, in the Senate of the United State: Friday, January 31, 1862, p. 16)

Character

"If I am to be shot at, I want no man to be in the way of the bullet." (*Andrew Johnson, President of the United States: His Life and Speeches*, Lillian Foster: 1866)

"Duties have been mine; consequences are God's." (*Life and Times of A. Johnson*. Written from a national standing, by a National Man, p.165)

1869 – 1877

Ulysses S. Grant

God

"Leave the matter of religion to the family altar, the church and the private school, supported entirely by private contributions. Keep the church and state forever separate." (Speech to the Society of the Army of Tennessee; archive.org.: 1875)

"Labor disgraces no man; unfortunately, you occasionally find men who disgrace labor." (Biography/Personal Quotes)

"There never was a time when, in my opinion, some way could not be found to prevent the drawing of the sword."

1877 – 1881

Rutherford B. Hayes

Character

"I hope you will be benefitted by your churchgoing. Where the habit does not Christianize, it generally civilizes. That is reason enough for supporting churches, if there were no higher." (*Diary and Letters of Rutherford Birchard Hayes*: *Nineteenth President of the United States,* Rutherford B. Hayes: 1922-1926)

"Unjust attacks on public men do them more good than unmerited praise." (*Diary and Letters of Rutherford Birchard Hayes: Nineteenth President of the United States,* Rutherford B. Hayes: 1922-1926)

God

"Conscience is the authentic voice of God to you." (Letter to his son, Scott R. Hayes. *Diary and Letters of Rutherford Birchard*

Hayes: *Nineteenth President of the United States*, Rutherford B. Hayes: 1922-1926)

"Must swear off from swearing. Bad habit." (Conspicuous Gallantry: *Civil Ward Diary and Letters of Rutherford B. Hayes*, p. 249, Big Byte Books)

Government

"To vote is like the payment of a debt, a duty never to be neglected, if its performance is possible." (Biography/Personal Quotes)

"Hundreds of laws of Congress and the state legislatures are in the interest of these men and against the interest of workingmen." (*Diary and Letters of Rutherford Birchard Hayes: Nineteenth President of the United States*, Rutherford B. Hayes: 1922-1926)

1881 – 1881

James A. Garfield

"I never meet a ragged boy in the street without feeling that I may owe him a salute, for I know not what possibilities may be buttoned up under his coat."

"If wrinkles must be written on our brow, let them not be written on our heart. The spirit should not grow old."

"There are men and women who make the world better just by being the kind of people they are. They have the gift of kindness or courage or loyalty or integrity. It really matters very little whether they are behind the wheel of a truck or running a business or bringing up a family. They teach the truth by living it."

Government

"It would be unjust to our people and dangerous to our institutions to apply a portion of revenues of the nation or of

P. J. Green

the States to the support of sectarian schools." (*The Works of James Abram Garfield*, Volume 2, p. 783)

"The chief duty of government is to keep the peace and stand out of the sunshine of the people."

1881 – 1885

Chester A. Arthur

"There are very many characteristics which go into making a model civil servant. Prominent among them are probity, industry, good sense, good habits, good temper, patience, order, courtesy, tack, self-reliance, many deference to superior officers, and many considerations for inferiors."

"Where you stand depends where you sit."

"Since I came here I have learned that Chester A. Arthur is one man and the President of the United States is another."

"No higher proof exists of the strength of popular government than, though the chosen of the people be struck down, his constitutional successor is peacefully installed without shock or strain."

1885 - 1889
1893 – 1897

Grover Cleveland

God

"I know there is a Supreme Being who rules the affairs of men and whose goodness and mercy have always followed the American people, and I know He will not turn from us now if we humbly and reverently seek His powerful aid." (Grover Cleveland: United States, President: 1885-1889)

"All must admit that the reception of the teachings of Christ results in the purest patriotism, in the most scrupulous fidelity to public trust, and in the best type of citizenship." (Addresses, State Papers and Letters)

Government

"Our citizens have the right to protection from the incompetency of public employees who hold their places solely as the reward of partisan service." (Grover Cleveland: United States, President: 1885-1889)

"What is the use of being elected or re-elected unless you stand for something? (*An Honest President*, H. Paul Jeffers: 2000)

"A truly American sentiments recognizes the dignity of labor and the fact that honor lies in honest toil." (Addresses, State Papers and Letters)

"Officeholders are the agents of the people, not their masters." (Grover Cleveland: United States, President: 1885-1889)

1889 – 1893

Benjamin Harrison

Flag

"That one flag encircles us with its folds today, the unrivaled object of our loyal love." (Public Papers and Addresses of Benjamin Harrison)

God

"We Americans have no commission from God to police the world." (Public Papers and Addresses of Benjamin Harrison)

Cheap Labor

"I pity the man who wants a coat so cheap that the man or woman who produces the cloth will starve in the process." (Rain Still Follows Him: The President's Vermont Trip Marked by Storms. Speech in Rutland, Vermont, reported in The New York Times: August 29, 1891 issue, p. 5)

1897 – 1901

William McKinley

Government Spending

"The best way for the Government to maintain its credit is to pay as it goes—not by resorting to loans, but by keeping out of debt through an adequate income secured by a system of taxation, external or internal, or both."

"If revenues are to remain as now, the only relief that can come must be from decreased expenditures. But the present must not become the permanent condition of the Government. It has been our uniform practice to retire, not increase our outstanding obligations, and this polity must again be resumed and vigorously enforced." (First Inaugural Address)

Cheap Labor = Cheap Goods

"I do not prize the word 'cheap.' It is not a badge of honor. It is

P. J. Green

a symbol of despair. Cheap prices make for cheap goods; cheap
goods make for cheap men; and cheap men make for a cheap
country."

1901 – 1909

Theodore Roosevelt

Old Age

"Old age is like everything else. To make a success of it, you've got to start young." (*Theodore Roosevelt on Bravery: Lessons from the Most Courageous Leader of the Twentieth Century*, p.7, Skyhorse Publishing, Inc.)

Positive Quotes

"Every thinking man, when he thinks, realizes that the teachings of the Bible are so interwoven and entwined with our whole civic and social life." (Theodore Roosevelt's Proclamation of a National Day of Thanksgiving and Prayer: 1908)

"We have room in this country for but one flag, the Stars and Stripes!" (The foes of our own household: The great adventure. Letters to his children)

"This country has nothing to fear from the crooked man who fails. We put him in jail. It is the crooked man who succeeds who is a threat to this country." (*The Bully Pulpit: A Teddy Roosevelt Book of Quotations*, p.72, Taylor Trade Publications)

1909-1913

William Howard Taft

"The President cannot make clouds to rain and cannot make the corn to grow. He cannot make business good, although when these things occur, political parties do claim some credit for the good things that have happened in this way." (*William Howard Taft: Essential Writings and Addresses*, p.150, Fairleigh Dickinson Univ Press)

"I think I might as well give up being a candidate. There are so many people in the country who don't like me." (Biography/Personal Quotes)

"Don't worry over what the newspapers say. I don't. Why should anyone else? I told the truth to the newspaper correspondents—but when you tell the truth to them they are at sea." (*The Life and Time of William Howard Taft*, Henry F. Pringle: 1939)

"No tendency is quite so strong in human nature as the desire to lay down rules of conduct for other people." (*Mr. Capone*, Robert J. Schoenberg: 1992)

"I am president now, and tired of being kicked around." (Biography/Personal Quotes)

"Enthusiasm for a cause sometimes warps judgement." (Peace, patriotic and religious speech by President Taft: delivered during his administration)

1913 – 1921

Woodrow Wilson

God

"Our civilization cannot survive materially unless it be redeemed spiritually with the Spirit of Christ."

Character

"You are not here merely to make a living. You are here in order to enable the world to live more amply, with greater vision, with a finer spirit of hope and achievement. You are here to enrich the world, and you impoverish yourself if you forget the errand." (*Selected Addresses and Public Paper of Woodrow Wilson*, p. 15, The Minerva Group, Inc.)

Military

"The only use of an obstacle is to be overcome. All that an obstacle does with brave men is, not to frighten them, but to challenge them." (The Public Papers of Woodrow Wilson: 1913-1917)

Government

"America was established not to create wealth but to realize a vision, to realize an ideal—to discover and maintain liberty among men."

"I would rather belong to a poor nation that was free than to a rich nation had ceased to be in love with liberty." (Positive Quotes about Woodrow Wilson)

"The government, which was designed for the people has got into the hands of the bosses and their employers, the special interests. An invisible empire has been set up above the forms of democracy." (*Woodrow Wilson: The Essential Political Writings*, p. 117, Lexington Books)

"Every man who takes office in Washington either grows or swells, and when I give a man an office, I watch him carefully to see whether he is growing or swelling."

"If there are men in this country big enough to own the government of the United States, they are going to own it."

(Important Addresses and Statements Delivered Between 1941 and 1952.)

"I do not want a government that will take care of me, I want a government that will make other men take their hands off me, so I can take care of myself." (*Woodrow Wilson: Essential Writings and Speeches of the Scholar-president*, p. 359, NYU Press)

"Since I entered politics, I have chiefly had men's views confided to me privately. Some of the biggest men in the United States, in the field of commerce and manufacture, are afraid of somebody, are afraid of something. They know that there is a power somewhere so organized, so subtle, so watchful, so interlocked, so complete, so pervasive, that they had better not speak above their breath when they speak in condemnation of it."

"We are no longer a government by free opinion, no longer a government by conviction and the vote of the majority, but a government by the opinion and the duress of small groups of dominant men." (*The New Freedom: A Call for the Emancipation of the Generous Energies of a People*, Woodrow Wilson, p. 13: 1913)

"The government, which was designed for the people, has got into the hands of the bosses and their employers, the special interests. An invisible empire has been set up above the forms of democracy." (*Woodrow Wilson: The Essential Political Writings*, p. 117, Lexington Books).

"I am a most unhappy man. I have unwittingly ruined my country. A great industrial nation is controlled by its system of credit. Our system of credit is concentrated. The growth of the nation, therefore, and all our activities are in the hands of a few men. We have come to be one of the worst ruled, one of the most completely controlled and dominated governments in the civilized world—no longer a government by free opinion, no longer, a government by conviction and the vote of the majority, but a government by the opinion and duress of a small group of dominant men."

"I have never considered a difference of opinion in politics, in

religion, in philosophy, as cause for withdrawing from a friend."
(AZQuotes.com)

Quotes about Woodrow Wilson

"In the Lord's Prayer, the first petition is for daily bread. No one can worship God or love his neighbor on an empty stomach."

Flag

Inaugural address

"The things that the flag stands for were created by the experiences of a great people. Everything that it stands for was written by their lives. The flag is the embodiment, not of sentiment, but of history."

"The flag is the embodiment, not of sentiment, but of history."

1921-1923

Warren G. Harding

God

"It is my conviction that the fundamental trouble with the people of the United States is that they have gotten too far away from Almighty God." (Pictures Harding as Man of Prayer. Quoted by Bishop William F. Anderson. The New York Times: April 2, 1922)

Government, Taxes

"I don't know what to do or where to turn in this taxation matter. Somewhere there must be a book that tells all about it, where I could go to straighten it out in my mind. But I don't know where the book is, and maybe I couldn't read it if I found it. (*The Shadow of Blooming Grove: Warren G. Harding in His Times*, Francis Russell: 1968)

Character

"I have no trouble with my enemies. I can take care of my enemies in a fight. But my friends, my goddamned friends, they're the ones who keep me walking the floor at nights!" (AZQuotes.com)

1923 – 1929

Calvin Coolidge

Military

"America seeks no earthly empire built on blood and force. No ambition, no temptation, lures her to thought of foreign dominions. America's "legions which she sends forth are armed, not with the sword, but with the cross." (Inaugural address of President Coolidge: March 4, 1925)

Government, taxes

"Any oppression laid upon the people by excessive taxation, any disregard of their right to hold and enjoy the property which they have rightfully acquired, would be fatal to freedom. A government which lays taxes on the people not required by urgent public necessity and sound public policy is not a protector of liberty, but an instrument of tyranny." (Speech given on August 1, 1930. Remarks made at Meeting of the

Business Organization of the Government in Memorial Continental Hall: June 30, 1924)

Senate

"I soon found that the Senate had but one fixed rule, subject to exceptions of course, which was to the effect that the Senate would do anything it wanted to do whenever it wanted to do it. When I had learned that, I did not waste much time with the other rules, because they were seldom applied." (*Autobiography of Calvin Coolidge,* pg. 162)

"If the Senate has any weakness it is because the people have sent to that body men lacking the necessary ability and character to perform the proper functions. But that is not the fault of the Senate. It cannot choose its own members but has to work with what is sent to it." (*Autobiography of Calvin Coolidge*, p. 163)

Government Spending and Taxes

"Nothing is easier than spending the public money. It does not appear to belong to anybody. The temptation is overwhelming to bestow it on somebody." (Readers Digest: June 1960)

"Every dollar expended must be made in the light of all our national resources and all our national needs." (At Memorial Continental Hall: June 30, 1924)

"The society which is satisfied is lost." (*The Price of Freedom*, p. 196)

In Coolidge's 1925 inaugural address.

"I favor the policy of economy, not because I wish to save money, but because I wish to save people. The men and women of this country who toil are the ones who bear the cost of the Government. Every dollar that we carelessly waste means that their life will be so much the more meager. Every dollar that we prudently save means that their life will be so much the more abundant."

Character

"Success comes to people who are not considering the narrow question of what they are paid for, but the broad question of what they can do to be helpful. It is that attitude which leads to the promotion of the individual, the profit of the business and the prosperity of the nation." (August 1, 1930)

"One with the law is a majority." (Speech: July 27, 1920)

"I know very well what it means to awake in the night and realize that the rent is coming due, wondering where the money is coming from with which to pay it. The only way I know of escape from that constant tragedy is to keep expenses low enough so that something may be saved to meet the day when earnings may be small." (*Autobiography of Calvin Coolidge*, p. 94)

1929 – 1933

Herbert Hoover

Humanity

"I am willing to pledge myself that if the time should ever come that the voluntary agencies of the country together with the local and state governments are unable to find resources with which to prevent hunger and suffering I will ask the aid of every resource of the Federal Government I have the faith in the American people that such a day will not come." (United States, President: 1929-1933)

Government

"When there is a lack of honor in government, the morals of the whole people are poisoned." (Addresses Upon the American Road: 1950-1955)

"Older men declare war. But it is youth that must fight and die. And it is youth who must inherit the tribulation, the sorrow, and the triumphs that are the aftermath of war." (Speech, Republican National Convention, Chicago: June 27, 1944)

"The only trouble with capitalism is capitalists; they're too damn greedy." *(The Wit and Wisdom of Herbert Hoover: A compilation of Many of His Quotations*, Vantage Press)

"Freedom requires that government keep the channels of competition and opportunity open, prevent monopolies, economic abuse and combination." (Addresses Upon the American Road)

"The budget should be balanced not by more taxes, but by reduction of follies." (American ideals and the New Deal)

"My country owes me nothing. It gave me, as it gives every boy and girl, a chance. It gave me schooling, independence of action, opportunity for service and honor. (Letter to Senator George H. Moses: June 14, 1928. *The Memoirs of Herbert Hoover*, volume 2, p. 195)

"Freedom is the open window through which pours the sunlight of the human spirit and human dignity." (*The Wit and Wisdom of Herbert Hoover: A Compilation of Many of His Quotations*, Vantage Press)

1933 – 1945

Franklin D. Roosevelt

Character and Our Youth

"We cannot always build the future for our youth, but we can build our youth for the future." (Address at University of Pennsylvania: September 20, 1940)

"Repetition does not transform a lie into a truth." (Radio Address to the New York Herald Tribune Forum: October 26, 1939)

"The only thing we have to fear is fear itself." (First Inaugural Address: March 4, 1933)

"When you see a rattlesnake poised to strike, you do not wait until he has struck before you crush him." (Fireside Chat: September 11, 1941)

"We all know that books burn—yet we have the greater knowledge that books cannot be killed by fire. People die, but books never die. No man and no force can abolish memory. In this war, we know, books are weapons." (Message, American Booksellers Association: April 23, 1942)

Government

"I should like to have it said of my first Administration that in it the forces of selfishness and of lust for power met their match. I should like to have it said of my second Administration that in it these forces met their master." (Speech, Madison Square Garden: October 31, 1936)

"The test of our progress is not whether we add more to the abundance of those who have much; it is whether we provide enough for those who have too little." (Second Inaugural Address: January 20, 1937)

"We must especially beware of that small group of selfish men who would clip the wings of the American Eagle in order to feather their own nests. (The Four Freedoms: January 6, 1941)

"Let us never forget that government is ourselves and not an alien power over us. The ultimate rulers of our democracy are not a President and Senators and Congressmen and Government officials but the voters of this country." (Franklin D. Roosevelt, Address at Marietta, Ohio: July 8 1938)

"The only limit to our realization of tomorrow will be our doubts of today." (Undelivered address for Jefferson Day: April 13, 1945, final lines, in Public Papers, 1950, vol. 13, p. 616)

"In our democracy officers of the government are the servants, and never the master of the people." (Public Papers of the

Presidents of the United States: Franklin D. Roosevelt: 1941, Vol 10", p. 40)

"Democracy cannot succeed unless those who express their choice are prepared to choose wisely. The real safeguard of democracy, therefore is education." (Public Papers of the Presidents of the United States: Franklin D. Roosevelt: 1941, Vol 7, p. 538)

"We look forward to a world founded by 4 essential freedoms:

Speech and expression

Worship God

From want

From fear."

Annual Message to Congress, January 6, 1944.

"We know now that government by the organized money is just as dangerous as government by organized mob." (Public Papers of the Presidents of the United States: Franklin D. Roosevelt: 1936, Vol 5, p. 538)

Military, War, Veterans

"We, too born to freedom, and believing in freedom, are willing to fight to maintain freedom. We, and all others who believe as deeply as we do would rather die on our feet than live on our knees." (On receiving the degree of Doctor of Civil Law from Oxford University: June 19, 1941)

"We have learned that we cannot live alone, at peace; that our own well-being is dependent on the well-being of other nations, far away. We have learned that we must live as men, and not as ostriches, nor as dogs in the manger. We have learned to be citizen of the world, members of the human community." (Fourth Inaugural Address: January 20, 1945)

Prayer by Roosevelt on June 6, 1944

"Last night, when I spoke with you about the fall of Rome, I knew at that moment that troops of the United States and our Allies were crossing the Channel in another and greater operation. It has come to pass with success thus far."

"And so, in this poignant hour, I ask you to join with me in prayer."

"They will need Thy blessings. Their road will be long and hard. For the enemy is strong. He may hurl back our forces. Success may not come with rushing speed, but we shall return again and again; and we know that by Thy grace, and by the righteousness of our cause, our sons will triumph."

"They will be sore tried, by night and by day, without rest—until the victory is won. The darkness will be rent by noise and flame. Men's souls will be shaken with the violence's of war."

"For these men are lately drawn from the ways of peace. They fight not for the lust of conquest. They fight to end conquest. They fight to liberate. They fight to let justice arise, and tolerance and good-will among all people. They yearn but for the end of battle, for their return to the haven of home."

"Some will never return. Embrace these, Father, and receive them. Thy heroic servants into Thy kingdom."

"With thy blessings, we shall prevail over the unholy forces of our enemy. Help us to conquer the apostles of greed and racial arrogances. Lead us to the saving of our country, and with our sister nations into a world unity that will spell a sure peace—a peace invulnerable to the scheming's of unworthy men. And a peace that will let all men live in freedom, reaping the just rewards of their honest toil. Thy will be done, Almighty God. Amen"

1945 – 1953

Harry S. Truman

God

"We believe that all men are created equal because they are created in the image of God." (Inaugural Address: January 20, 1949)

"We must not sink into pagan materialism." (At the 150th anniversary of Declaration of Independence)

"The strength of our country is the strength of its religious convictions. The foundations of our society and our government rest so much on the teachings of the Bible that it would be difficult to support them if faith in these teachings would cease to be practically universal in our country."

"In love alone—the love of God and the love of man—will be found the solution of all the ills which afflict the world today. Slowly, sometimes painfully, but always with increasing purpose, emerges the great message of Christianity: only with wisdom comes joy, and with greatness comes love."

"Peace is the goal of my life. I'd rather have lasting peace in the world than be President. I wish for peace, I work for peace and I pray for peace continually." (Lighting of the Christmas Tree)

"I wonder how far Moses would have gone if he had taken a poll in Egypt? What would Jesus Christ have preached if He had taken a poll in the land of Israel? Where would the Reformation have gone if Martin Luther had taken a poll?" (Harry S. Truman in his own words, by William Hillman)

Government

"A man who is influenced by the polls or is afraid to make decisions which make him unpopular is not a man to represent the welfare of the country." (1946-52: *Years of Trial and Hope*, p.243, New Word City)

"Once a government is committed to the principle of silencing the voice of opposition, it has only one way to go, and that is down the path of increasingly repressive measures, until it becomes a source of terror to all its citizens and creates a country where everyone lives in fear." (Harry S. Truman: Containing the Public Messages, Speeches and Statements of the President: 1945-1953)

"A leader is the man who has the ability to get other people to do what they don't want to do, and like it." (Harry S. Truman: 1945, *Year of Decision*, p. 145, New Word City)

"Being a President is like riding a tiger. A man has to keep on riding or be swallowed." (Memoirs: 1955, vol. II, *Years of Trial and Hope*, chapter 1)

"Most of the problems a President has to face have their roots in the past." (Memoirs: 1955, vol. II, *Years of Trial and Hope*, chapter 1)

"To me, party platforms are contracts with the people." (Memoirs: 1955, vol. II, *Years of Trial and Hope*, chapter 13)

In poor health—2 months before his death.

"The fundamental basis of this nation's laws was given to Moses on the Mount. The fundamental basis of our Bill of Rights comes from the teachings we get from Exodus and St. Matthew, from Isaiah and St. Paul. we will finally end up with a totalitarian government which does not believe in rights for anybody except the State!"

Veterans

Our debt to the heroic men and valiant women in the service of our country can never be repaid. They have earned our undying gratitude. America will never forget their sacrifices." (United States, President: 1945-1953)

Character

"America was not built on fear. America was built on courage, on imagination and an unbeatable determination to do the job at hand." (*The Quotable Harry S. Truman*, Anderson, S.C.: Droke House, distributed by Grosset and Dunlap)

Historical Americans

Benjamin Franklin

God

"Here is my Creed. I believe in one God, creator of the Universe. That he governs it by his Providence. That he ought to be worshiped. That the most acceptable service we render him is doing good to his other children. That the soul of Man is immortal will be treated with justice in another life respecting its conduct in this." (*The Life of Benjamin Franklin*: written by Himself)

"Fear God, and your enemies will fear you." (*The Way to Wealth and Poor Richard's Almanac*, Nayika Publishing)

"Rebellion to tyrants is obedience to God." (Pennsylvania Evening Post: December 14, 1775)

"I have lived, sir, a long time; and the longer I live the more convincing proofs I see of this truth, that God governs in the affairs of men! And if a sparrow cannot fall to the ground without his notice, is it probable that an empire can rise without his aid? We have been assured, sir, in the sacred writings, that except the lord build the house, they labor in vain that build it. I firmly believe this; and I also believe that without his concurring aid, we shall succeed in this political building no better than the builders of Babel: we shall be divided by our little partial local interest, our projects will be confounded and we ourselves shall become a reproach and a byword down to future ages." (At the beginning of the Constitutional Convention, Pennsylvania: June 28, 1787).

"God helps them that help themselves." (Poor Richard's Almanack)

Government

"Whoever would overthrow the liberty of a nation must begin by subduing the freedom of speech, a thing terrible to traitors." (*The Real Benjamin Franklin*)

"I wish the bald eagle had not been chosen as the representative of our country; he is a bird of bad moral character; like those among men who live by sharping and robbing, he is generally poor, and often very lousy."

The way to secure peace is to be prepared for war. They that are on their guard, and appear ready to receive their adversaries, are in much less danger of being attacked, than the supine, secure, and negligent." (*Memories of the Life and Writing of Benjamin Franklin*, p. 235)

"These unhappy times call for the building of plans...that build from the bottom up and not from the top down, that put their faith once more in the forgotten man at the bottom of the economic pyramid." (Radio address: April 7,1932)

"In free governments the rulers are the servants, and the people their superiors and sovereigns. (*The Real Benjamin Franklin*)

Character

"If by the liberty of the press means the liberty of affronting, calumniating and defaming one another, I, for my part, own myself willing to part with my share of it." (An Account of the Supremist Court of Judicature in Pennsylvania, viz. The Court of the Press: September 12, 1789)

"Who is wise? He that learns from everyone. Who is powerful? He that governs his passions. Who is rich? He that is content. Who is that? Nobody." (Poor Richard's Almanac: 1733)

"A little house well filled, a little field well tilled, and a little wife well willed are great riches." (Poor Richard's Almanac: 1735)

"If you would not be forgotten, as soon as you are dead and rotten, either write things worth reading, or do things worth the writing." (Poor Richard's Almanac: 1738)

"When men are employed, they are best contented; for on the days they worked they were good-natured and cheerful, and with the consciousness of having done a good day's work, they spent the evening jollily; but on our idle days they were mutinous and quarrelsome." (Poor Richard's Almanac: 1733)

"Keep your eyes wide open before marriage, half shut afterwards." (Poor Richard's Almanac :1738)

"Dost thou love Life? Then do not squander Time; for that's the stuff life is made of. Lost time is never found again." (Poor Richard's Almanac: 1748)

"The cat in gloves catches no mice." (Poor Richard's Almanac: 1754)

"We must all hang together, or assuredly we shall all hang separately." (At the signing of the Declaration of Independence: July 4, 1776)

"I hope our people will keep up their courage. I have no doubt of their finally succeeding by the blessing of God." (Letter to an unknown correspondent: Oct. 25, 1776)

"Beware of the young doctor and the old barber" (*Benjamin Wit and Wisdom* from Poor Richard's Almanack, p. 27, Courier)

"Make yourself sheep and the wolves will eat you." (*The Completed Autobiography of Benjamin Franklin*, p. 108, Regnery Publishers)

"You may delay, but time will not." (*Benjamin Franklin Wit and Wisdom*, p.43, Peter Pauper Press, Inc.)

Samuel Adams

"He who made all men hath made the truths necessary to human happiness obvious to all." (Speech at the State House, Philadelphia: August 1, 1776)

"Our children may have their minds impressed with a strong sense of the duties they owe to their God." (Address to the Legislature of Massachusetts: January 30, 1787)

"Religion in a family is at once its brightest ornament and its best security." (Letter to Thomas Wells: November 22, 1780)

"Mankind are governed more by their feelings than by reason." (In J.N. Rakove, *The Beginnings of National Politics:* 1979, p.92)

Frederick Douglas

"It is easier to build strong children than to repair broken men.

Abigail Adams

Wife of John Adams, 2nd president of U.S.

During conflict with Britain, she wrote:

"The race is not to the swift, nor the battle to the strong; but the God of Israel is He that giveth strength and power unto His people. Trust in Him at all times, ye people, pour out your hearts before him; God is a refuge for us."

Alexander Hamilton

"All communities divide themselves into the few and the many. The first are the rich and the wellborn, the other the mass of the people."

"In politics, as in religion, it is equally absurd to aim at making proselytes by fire and sword. Heresies in either can rarely be cured by persecution." (Alexander Hamilton: Federalist No. 1: October 27, 1787)

"A garden, you know, is a very usual refuge of a disappointed politician. Accordingly, I have purchased a few acres about nine miles from town, have built a house, and am cultivating a garden." (Correspondence: 1795-1804, 1777, 1791. Letters of H.G. 1789. Address to public creditors. 1790. Vindication of funding system: 1791, p.551)

Patrick Henry
American Patriot

God

"We are not weak if we make a proper use of those means which the God of Nature has placed in our power. The battle, sir, is not to the strong alone; it is to the vigilant, the active, and the brave." (Speech in Virginia Convention: March 23, 1775)

"There is a just God who presides over the destinies of nations, and who will raise up friends to fight our battles for us. The battle, sire, is not to the strong alone; it is to the vigilant, and active, the brave." (Virginia Conventions: March 23, 1775)

"Being a Christian is a character which I prize far above all this world has or can boast." (*First-Person: The Faith of Patrick Henry* Kelly Boggs: June 27, 2014)

Last Will and Testament

"This is all the inheritance I can give my dear family. The religion of Christ can give them one which will make them rich indeed."

"My most cherished possession I wish I could leave you is my faith in Jesus Christ, for with him and nothing else you can be happy, but without him and with all else you'll never be happy."

7/12/1804 at his death:

"I have a tender reliance on the mercy of the Almighty, through the merits of the Lord Jesus Christ. I am a sinner. I look to Him for mercy; pray for me."

George Washington Carver

"Education is the key to unlock the golden door of freedom." (*George Washington Carver: In His Own Words*, p.62, University of Missouri Press)

"No individual has any right to come into the world and go out of it without leaving behind him distinct and legitimate reason for having passed through it." (*George Washington Carver: In His Own Words*, p.1, University of Missouri Press)

Mark Twain

Character

"Keep away from people who try to belittle your ambitions. Small people always do that, but the really great make you feel that you, too, can become great." (*Mark Twain at your Fingertips: A Book of Quotations*, p. 354, Courier Corporation)

"Some people get an education without going to college. The rest get it after they get out." (*Mark Twain on Common Sense: Timeless Advice and Words of Wisdom from America's Most-Revered Humorist*, p.13, Skyhorse Publishing, Inc.)

"Whenever you find yourself on the side of the majority, it is time to pause and reflect." (*The Wit and Wisdom of Mark Twain*, p.97, Chartwell)

"If you tell the truth, you don't have to remember anything." (*Mark Twain's Own Autobiography: The Chapters from the North American Review*, p.43, University of Wisconsin Press)

Thomas A. Edison

"Opportunity is missed by most people because it is dressed in overalls and looks like work." (*An Enemy Called Average*, John L. Mason: 1990)

"If we did all the things we are capable of doing, we would literally astound ourselves." (*Motivating Humans: Goals, Emotions, and Personal Agency Beliefs*, Martin E. Ford: 1992)

"Show me a thoroughly satisfied man—and I will show you a failure." (*The Diary and Sunday Observations of Thomas Alva Edison*, Thomas A. Edison: 1948)

Will Rogers

"Everything is funny as long as it is happening to somebody else." (The Illiterate Digest: 1924, p. 131)

"I never met a man I didn't like." (Address, Boston: June 1930)

"I not only "don't choose to run" for President no matter how bad the country will need a comedian at that time." (Syndicated newspaper article: June 28, 1931)

"My forefathers didn't come over on the Mayflower, but they met the boat." (He was of Indian descent.)

Regarding Congress:

"I don't think either one of them knows what it's all about, to be honest with you. Both sides are doing nothing but just looking towards the next election." (*Radio broadcasts of Will Rogers*, Oklahoma State University Press)

"The difference between a Republican and a Democrat is that the Democrat is a cannibal, they live off each other, while the Republicans live off the Democrats." (Will Rogers Speaks. Over 1,000 Timeless Quotations for Public Speakers and Writers, Politicians, Comedians, Browsers)

"This country has come to feel the same when Congress is in session as when the baby gets hold of a hammer." (Will Rogers' Daily Telegrams: The Coolidge years: 1926-1929", Will Rogers Heritage Trust)

"America has the best politicians money can buy." (Will Rogers Speaks: Over 1,000 Timeless Quotations for Public Speakers, M Evans & Company)

"I don't make jokes. I just watch the government and report the facts." (In Saturday Review: August 25, 1962)

"The short memories of the American voters is what keeps our politicians in office." (*Will Rogers' World: America's Foremost Political Humorist Comments on the Twenties and Thirties— and Eighties and Nineties. P. 86, Rowman and Littlefield)

Ralph Waldo Emerson

"We are all inventors, each sailing out on a voyage of discovery, guided each by a private chart, of which there is no duplicate. The world is all gates, all opportunities." (*The Later Lectures of Ralph Waldo Emerson*, 1843-1871, p.340, University of Georgia Press)

To finish the moment, to find the journey's end in every step of the road, to live the greatest number of good hours, is wisdom." (*The Portable Emerson*: New Edition, p.207, Penguin)

Thomas Paine

Common Sense, 1776

"The reformation was preceded by the discovery of America, as if the Almighty graciously meant to open a sanctuary to the persecuted."

"What we obtain too cheap, we esteem too lightly." (The American Crises, No. 1: December 19, 1776)

"Those who expect to reap the blessings of freedom, must, like men, undergo the fatigues of supporting it." (The American Crisis, No. 4, September 12, 1777)

Albert Einstein:

"My comprehension of God comes from a deeply felt conviction of a superior intelligence that reveals itself in the knowable world." (*The Ultimate Quotable Einstein*, p. 324, Princeton University Press)

"The world will not be destroyed by those who do evil, but by those who watch them without doing anything."

John Hancock

First declaration signer—Governor Of Massachusetts:

"That all may bow to the scepter of our Lord Jesus Christ and that the whole Earth may be filled with his glory.

God

"It is recommended to the good people of this colony of all denominations, that Thursday the 11th day of May next be set apart as a Day of Public Humiliation, Fasting and Prayer to confess their sins." (April 15, 1775)

"A chip on the shoulder is too heavy a piece of baggage to carry through life." (Biography/Personal quotes)

Audie Murphy

WWII Medal of Honor – saved many American lives

Asked the true meaning of America:

"It's in a Texas rodeo, in a policeman's badge, in the sound of laughing children, in a political rally, in a newspaper. In all these things, and many more, you'll find America. In all these things, you'll find freedom. And freedom is what America means to the world."

Joseph Story

Supreme Court Justice:

"Thank God! I—I also—am an American!" (On Mr. Justice Story: September 12, 1845)

There never has been a period in which the Common Law did not recognize Christianity as lying its foundations." (Harvard Speech: 1829)

Benjamin Rush

Wrote letter in 1790's in Defense of the Bible in all schools in America:

"I lament that we waste so much time and money in punishing crimes and take so little pains to prevent them...By withholding the knowledge of (the Scriptures) from children, we deprive ourselves of the best means of awakening moral sensibility in their minds." (U.S. History Quotes About God and the Bible. Benjamin Rush: On the Mode of Education Proper in a Republic: 1806)

Sergeant. Alvin York

At Tomb of Unknown Soldier, 1941

When asked "What did war get you?"

"The thing they forget is that liberty and freedom and democracy are so very precious that you do not fight to win them once and then stop. Liberty and freedom and democracy are prizes awarded only to those peoples who fight to win them and the keep fighting eternally to hold them."

Noah Webster

American English—language spelling reformer

1828 in the preface to his American Dictionary:

Noah Wester, The History of the United States and US History Quotes About God and the Bible

God

"Let it be impressed on your mind that God commands you to choose for rulers just men who will rule in the fear of God. (Exodus 18:21) If the citizens neglect their duty and place unprincipled men in office, the government will soon be corrupted." (Noah Webster—American English—language spelling reformer 1828 in the preface to his American Dictionary: Noah Wester, The History of the United States and US History Quotes About God and the Bible)

In his American Dictionary of the English Language creation as follows: "Creation especially, the act of bringing this world into existence, Romans 1 Creature every being besides, the Creator."

Jefferson Memorial

"I tremble for my country when I reflect that God is just; that his justice cannot sleep forever." (Article: U.S. Presidents speak out! U.S. History Quotes About God and the Bible)

Daniel Webster

Senator

God

"Whatever makes men good Christians, makes them good citizens." (Speech at Plymouth, Massachusetts: December 22, 1820)

"It is my living sentiment, and by the blessing of God it shall be my dying sentiment—Independence now and Independence forever." (Discourse in Commemoration of Adams and Jefferson, Faneuil Hall, Boston: August 2, 1826)

"If the power of the Gospel is not felt throughout the length and breadth of the land, anarchy and misrule, degradation and misery, corruption and darkness will reign without mitigation or end."

"I regard it (the Constitution) as the work of the purest patriots and wisest statesman that ever existed, aided by the smiles of a benign Providence; it almost appears a "Divine interposition in our behalf the hand that destroys our Constitution rends our Union asunder forever."

"Hold on, my friends, to the Constitution of your country and the government established under it. Leave evils which exist in some parts of the country, but which are beyond your control, to the all-wise direction of an over-ruling Providence. Perform those duties which are present, plain and positive. Respect the laws of your country." (Letters to Dr. William B. Gooch of West Dennis, Massachusetts, in 1851. The Bay State Monthly: 1898)

"God grants liberty only to those who love it and are always ready to guard and defend it." (Speech: June 3, 1834)

Government

"Our destruction, should it come at all, will be from the inattention of the people to the concerns of their government, from their carelessness and negligence." (The Union Text Gook: Containing Selections from the Writings of D.W.; the Declaration of Independence; and Washington's Farewell Address, Etc., p.259)

Education

"Education is useless without the Bible." US History Quotes About God and the Bible. (Daniel Webster said this on the bicentennial Celebration of the landing of the Pilgrims at Plymouth Rock)

Beauty of Our Country

"The materials of wealth are in the earth, in the seas, and in their natural and unaided productions." (*The Great Speeches and Orations of Daniel Webster*, p.451, Beard Books)

Booker T. Washington

"I will permit no man to narrow and degrade my soul by making me hate him." (Autobiography by Booker T. Washington, Up from Slavery)

Martha Washington

Wrote a friend after losing a dear friend:

"I am still determined to be cheerful and happy, in whatever situation I may be; for I have also learned from experience that the greater part of our happiness or misery depends upon our dispositions, and not upon our circumstances."

Eleanor Roosevelt

Wartime Prayer

Dear Lord,

Lest I continue

My complacent way,

Help me to remember that somewhere,

Somehow out there

A man died for me today.

As long as there be ward,

I then must Ask and answer

Am I worth dying for?

God's Garden

Written about the Korean War

Author unknown
God looked around His garden,
And found an empty place
He then looked down upon the earth,
And saw your tired face.
He put His arms around you,
And lifted you to rest.
God's garden must be beautiful,
He always takes the best.
He knew that you were suffering.
He knew that you were in pain.
He knew that you would never,
Get well on earth again.
He saw the road was getting rough,
And the hills were hard to climb
So, he closed your weary eyelids,
And whispered, "peace be thing."
It broke our hearts to lose you,
But you didn't go alone.
For part of us went with you
The day god called you home.

West Point Cadet

Prayer for use by young Americans:

"Make us to choose the harder right instead of the easier wrong, and never to be content with a half-truth when the whole truth can be won."